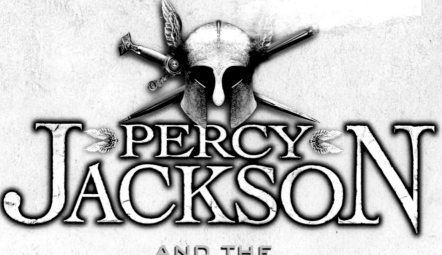

PERCY JACKSON

AND THE
TITAN'S CURSE

THE GRAPHIC NOVEL

BY

RICK RIORDAN

ADAPTED BY
ROBERT VENDITTI

ART BY
ATTILA FUTAK

COLOUR BY
GREGORY GUILHAUMOND

LETTERING BY
CHRIS DICKEY

RICK RIORDAN is the author of all the books in the *New York Times* No. 1 bestselling Percy Jackson series: *The Lightning Thief, The Sea of Monsters, The Titan's Curse, The Battle of the Labyrinth* and *The Last Olympian*. His other novels for children include the *New York Times* No. 1 bestselling series the Kane Chronicles (*The Red Pyramid, The Throne of Fire* and *The Serpent's Shadow*) and the Heroes of Olympus (*The Lost Hero, The Son of Neptune, The Mark of Athena* and *The House of Hades*). He lives in Boston, Massachusetts, with his wife and two sons. Learn more at www.rickriordanmythmaster.co.uk.

ROBERT VENDITTI is the *New York Times* bestselling author of *The Homeland Directive* and *The Surrogates*, as well as *The Surrogates: Flesh and Bone*. He also adapted the *New York Times* bestselling *Percy Jackson and the Lightning Thief: The Graphic Novel*, *Percy Jackson and the Sea of Monsters: The Graphic Novel* and *Blue Bloods: The Graphic Novel*. He lives in Atlanta, Georgia. Visit his website at www.robertvenditti.com.

ATTILA FUTAKI is the *New York Times* bestselling illustrator of *Percy Jackson and the Lightning Thief: The Graphic Novel* and *Percy Jackson and the Sea of Monsters: The Graphic Novel*. He also illustrated and coloured *Conan the Barbarian* (written by Victor Gischler) and *Severed* (written by Scott Snyder and Scott Tuft). Attila studied at the International School of Comics in Florence, Italy. He lives in Budapest, Hungary. Visit www.attilafutaki.blogspot.co.uk.

GREG GUILHAUMOND studied drawing and animation at the European School of Visual Arts. After graduating, he worked in web and graphic design while also doing illustrations for various role-playing games and magazines and producing underground comics. Greg provided the colours for *Severed*. *Percy Jackson and the Titan's Curse: The Graphic Novel* is his first book for children. He lives in Tours, France. Visit doublegarga.canalblog.com.

WESTOVER MILITARY ACADEMY.

BAR HARBOR, MAINE.

MY NAME'S PERCY.

DON'T WORRY. I'M GOING TO TAKE YOU SOMEWHERE SAFE.

WHISH

THUNK

AH!

FEAR NOT, **PERSEUS JACKSON.** MY POISON WILL NOT KILL YOU.

THOUGH THE **PAIN** MAY MAKE YOU WISH IT HAD.

NOW, ALL THREE OF YOU WILL COME WITH ME, OR I WILL SHOW YOU JUST HOW **ACCURATELY** I CAN SHOOT.

I WILL DELIVER THE PACKAGE SHORTLY.

UNFORTUNATELY, YOU ARE WANTED ALIVE. OTHERWISE YOU WOULD ALREADY BE DEAD.

WHO'D WANT *US*, DR. THORN?

MY BROTHER AND I...WE DON'T HAVE ANY FAMILY.

RANSOM? YOU HAVE NO IDEA WHAT IS HAPPENING, YOU INSUFFERABLE GIRL.

I WILL LET THE *GENERAL* ENLIGHTEN YOU. HE LOOKS FORWARD TO MEETING YOU.

YOU ARE ALL TO BE GIVEN THE OPPORTUNITY TO JOIN A GREAT ARMY. AND IF YOU CHOOSE *NOT* TO JOIN...

WELL, THERE ARE MANY MONSTROUS MOUTHS TO FEED. THE *GREAT STIRRING* IS UNDER WAY.

THE GREAT WHAT?

THE STIRRING OF MONSTERS. THE WORST OF THEM ARE NOW WAKING. THEY WILL CAUSE DESTRUCTION THE LIKES OF WHICH MORTALS HAVE NEVER KNOWN.

AND SOON WE SHALL HAVE THE MOST IMPORTANT MONSTER OF ALL--THE ONE THAT SHALL BRING ABOUT THE *DOWNFALL OF OLYMPUS*.

WE HAVE TO JUMP OFF THE CLIFF. IT'S OUR ONLY CHANCE. THE OCEAN *MUST* BE DOWN THERE SOMEWHERE.

SURE THING, KID-THAT-I-JUST-MET. IS THAT BEFORE OR AFTER THE "MONSTERS" DESTROY THE WORLD?

HAS EVERYONE GONE COMPLETELY *NUTS*?

SILENCE OR I'LL MAKE SURE YOUR NEXT UTTERANCE IS A PLEA FOR MERCY!

-=oof=-

WHAT?

UM...THANKS, ANNABETH.

FOR ZEUS!

YAH!

SCRIIITCH

YOUR PALTRY WOODLAND MAGIC IS NO MATCH FOR *ME*, SATYR!

THUNK

ROAR!

NO. IT CANNOT BE...

THIS IS NOT FAIR! DIRECT INTERFERENCE IS AGAINST THE ANCIENT LAWS!

NOT SO. THE HUNTING OF ALL WILD BEASTS IS WITHIN MY SPHERE.

AND YOU, *FOUL CREATURE*, ARE A WILD BEAST.

WHISH

THE GODLINGS ARE MINE!

SHWIP

SHWIP

SHWIP

GRRRR... VERY WELL. IF I CANNOT HAVE THE GODLINGS ALIVE, THEN I SHALL HAVE THEM *DEAD!*

NOT IF I HAVE SOMETHING TO SAY ABOUT IT!

RARRRI

CURSE YOU!

ANNABETH!

COME ON! WE HAVE TO HELP HER!

SHE IS BEYOND HELP.

CAN YOU NOT SENSE IT, SON OF POSEIDON? THERE IS *MAGIC* AT WORK. I DO NOT KNOW HOW OR WHY, BUT YOUR FRIEND HAS VANISHED.

VANISHED?! THEN LET'S *FIND* HER.

WHOA. *TIME OUT.* WHAT DID YOU JUST CALL HIM?

WHO *ARE* YOU PEOPLE?

I AM *ARTEMIS*, GODDESS OF THE HUNT. THESE ARE MY HUNTERS.

THE BETTER QUESTION, MY DEAR GIRL, IS WHO ARE *YOU*? WHO ARE YOUR PARENTS?

I'M BIANCA DI ANGELO, AND THIS IS MY BROTHER, NICO.

OUR PARENTS ARE DEAD. WE'RE ORPHANS.

NO. YOU ARE *HALF-BLOODS.*

ONE OF THY PARENTS WAS MORTAL, BUT THE OTHER WAS AN OLYMPIAN.

OLYMPIAN? LIKE A...GREEK GOD? YOU EXPECT ME TO BELIEVE THAT?

REMEMBER THAT BUS DRIVER WITH THE RAM'S HORNS? I *TOLD* YOU THAT WAS REAL!

AND LAST SUMMER, THERE WERE THOSE... THINGS...THAT TRIED TO ATTACK US IN THE ALLEY.

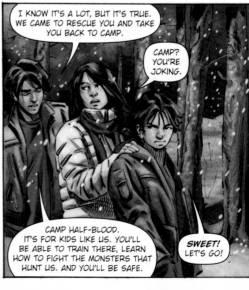

I KNOW IT'S A LOT, BUT IT'S TRUE. WE CAME TO RESCUE YOU AND TAKE YOU BACK TO CAMP.

CAMP? YOU'RE JOKING.

CAMP HALF-BLOOD. IT'S FOR KIDS LIKE US. YOU'LL BE ABLE TO TRAIN THERE, LEARN HOW TO FIGHT THE MONSTERS THAT HUNT US. AND YOU'LL BE SAFE.

SWEET! LET'S GO!

BUT WE JUST MET YOU GUYS. MY BROTHER AND I HAVE A LIFE HERE.

SORT OF...

I'M SORRY. REALLY. THERE ISN'T ANY OTHER WAY.

VERILY, THERE IS ANOTHER OPTION. FOR *HER*.

NO, THERE ISN'T! YOU'RE NOT GOING TO--

ENOUGH. WE WILL REST HERE FOR A FEW HOURS.

ZOË, RAISE THE TENTS AND SEE THAT THE WOUNDED ARE TENDED TO.

AND SEND SOME OF THE OTHERS TO RETRIEVE OUR GUESTS' BELONGINGS.

YES, MY LADY.

BIANCA, COME WITH ME. I WISH TO SPEAK WITH YOU IN PRIVATE.

THE *NERVE* OF THOSE HUNTERS!

I'M WITH YOU. THEY SHOULD BE HELPING US LOOK FOR ANNABETH.

OH, YOU'RE *WITH ME* NOW?

TOO BAD YOU WEREN'T WITH ME WHEN YOU DECIDED TO TAKE ON A MANTICORE ALL BY YOURSELF.

THIS WAS SUPPOSED TO BE *OUR* MISSION.

IF YOU'D WAITED FOR US, WE COULD'VE TAKEN HIM ON TOGETHER. AND MAYBE *ANNABETH* WOULD STILL BE HERE!

THINK ABOUT *THAT!*

THAT MAGIC SALVE SHOULD DO THE TRICK.

THANKS, GROVER. IT'S FEELING BETTER ALREADY.

ARGH! TAKE THAT!

YOU SURE HAVE A BUNCH OF THOSE FIGURINES, NICO. HOW LONG HAVE YOU BEEN COLLECTING THEM?

ABOUT A YEAR. I THINK. BEFORE THAT, I WAS INTO...

I DON'T REMEMBER. THAT'S WEIRD.

HEY! DOES ZEUS REALLY HAVE LIGHTNING BOLTS THAT DO *SIX HUNDRED* DAMAGE? CAN *POSEIDON*--

--THAT'S YOUR DAD, RIGHT?

HOW DOES HE MAKE HURRICANES?

I--

PERCY JACKSON.

LADY ARTEMIS WILL SPEAK WITH THEE.

FORGIVE MY HUNTERS IF THEY ARE GRUFF. IT IS VERY RARE THAT WE HAVE BOYS IN OUR CAMP.

AND THEY HAVE SEEN SO MANY YOUNG MAIDENS GO *ASTRAY*.

ASTRAY?

FORGET THEMSELVES. BECOME SILLY, PREOCCUPIED, INSECURE.

A RESULT OF BEING *SMITTEN* WITH BOYS.

OH. RIGHT.

I ASKED YOU HERE TO LEARN MORE ABOUT THE MANTICORE. BIANCA HAS REPORTED SOME OF THE...DISTURBING THINGS THE MONSTER SAID.

BUT SHE MAY NOT HAVE UNDERSTOOD THEM.

I'D LIKE TO HEAR THEM FROM YOU.

HE MENTIONED SOMETHING ABOUT "THE GENERAL."

THEN HE SAID THERE WAS A "GREAT STIRRING," AND THAT SOON THEY'D HAVE THE MONSTER THAT WOULD BRING ABOUT THE "DOWNFALL OF OLYMPUS."

AND HE THREATENED TO EAT US. BUT, YOU KNOW, *ALL* MONSTERS DO THAT.

THE *GENERAL*...? HOW COULD IT BE?

IT IS AS I FEARED.

I MUST FIND THIS CREATURE AND BRING IT BACK TO OLYMPUS BY WINTER SOLSTICE. IT WILL BE THE PROOF I NEED TO CONVINCE THE COUNCIL OF HOW MUCH DANGER WE ARE IN.

WE SHALL BEGIN THE HUNT AT ONCE, MY LADY.

NO. THIS TASK IS TOO DANGEROUS EVEN FOR THE HUNTERS. I MUST GO ALONE.

YOU AND THE OTHERS WILL GO TO CAMP HALF-BLOOD. CABIN EIGHT IS THE HUNTERS' TO USE BY RIGHT. AND PERHAPS THERE WILL BE *ONE MORE* OF YOU TO SHARE IT.

HAVE YOU MADE YOUR DECISION, BIANCA?

I...

WAIT. WHAT DECISION?

BIANCA HAS BEEN ASKED TO JOIN THE HUNT.

SWEAR LOYALTY TO ME, CHILD, AND YOU WILL BE GIVEN THE GIFT OF IMMORTALITY. DEATH MAY COME TO YOU ONLY IN BATTLE.

YOU MAY STILL SEE YOUR BROTHER FROM TIME TO TIME, BUT YOU WILL HAVE A NEW FAMILY. *US.*

ALL I ASK IN EXCHANGE IS THAT YOU FORSWEAR ROMANTIC LOVE FOREVER. YOU WILL NEVER GROW UP, NEVER BE MARRIED.

YOU WILL BE A MAIDEN ETERNALLY.

A NEW FAMILY...FREE OF RESPONSIBILITY.

I ACCEPT.

WELCOME, SISTER.

REMEMBER YOUR OATH. IT IS NOW YOUR LIFE.

WHAT ABOUT NICO?

HE'LL BE SAFE AT CAMP. YOU SAID SO YOURSELF.

I'M SORRY, PERCY. I KNOW IT'S SUDDEN, BUT I WANT THIS. *I REALLY DO.*

BREAK CAMP AT ONCE, ZOË. YOU MUST ALL HEAD TO LONG ISLAND.

I LEAVE YOU IN CHARGE OF THE HUNTERS IN MY STEAD. DO AS I WOULD DO.

YES, MY LADY.

DAWN APPROACHES. *FINALLY.*

HE IS SO LAZY DURING THE WINTER.

IT WOULD BE WISE IF YOU SHIELDED YOUR EYES. AT LEAST UNTIL HE PARKS.

UNTIL *WHO* PARKS?

ALLOW ME TO INTRODUCE MY TWIN BROTHER, *APOLLO.* GOD OF THE SUN.

AND *POETRY,* AMONG OTHER THINGS.

WAIT. I FEEL A HAIKU COMING ON. *-:ahem:-*

GREEN GRASS BREAKS THROUGH SNOW.

ARTEMIS WAITS FOR MY HELP.

I AM SO AWESOME.

WHAT'S UP, *LITTLE SIS?* YOU NEVER CALL. YOU NEVER WRITE. I WAS GETTING WORRIED!

I AM *NOT* YOUR "LITTLE" SISTER.

AND I AM FINE, BROTHER. BUT I HAVE SOME HUNTING TO DO ALONE. I NEED YOU TO TAKE MY COMPANIONS TO CAMP HALF-BLOOD.

NO SWEAT, SIS.

HI, LORD APOLLO.

HEY...THALIA, RIGHT? YOU USED TO BE A TREE, DIDN'T YOU? GLAD YOU'RE BACK. I HATE IT WHEN PRETTY GIRLS GET TURNED INTO TREES.

WELL, WE'D BETTER LOAD UP. RIDE ONLY GOES ONE WAY--WEST--AND IF YOU MISS IT, YOU MISS IT.

COOL CAR! BUT HOW'RE WE ALL GONNA FIT?

OH, RIGHT. I HATE TO CHANGE OUT OF SPORTS-CAR MODE, BUT I SUPPOSE...

CLICK

WOW! IS THIS *REALLY* THE SUN CHARIOT? HOW DOES IT WORK? I THOUGHT THE SUN WAS A BIG FIERY BALL OF GAS!

HEH. THAT RUMOR PROBABLY GOT STARTED BECAUSE ARTEMIS USED TO CALL *ME* A BIG FIERY BALL OF GAS.

SERIOUSLY, KID, IT'S NOT AN *ASTRONOMY* THING SO MUCH AS A *PHILOSOPHY* THING.

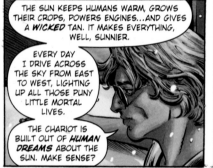

THE SUN KEEPS HUMANS WARM, GROWS THEIR CROPS, POWERS ENGINES...AND GIVES A *WICKED* TAN. IT MAKES EVERYTHING, WELL, SUNNIER.

EVERY DAY I DRIVE ACROSS THE SKY FROM EAST TO WEST, LIGHTING UP ALL THOSE PUNY LITTLE MORTAL LIVES.

THE CHARIOT IS BUILT OUT OF *HUMAN DREAMS* ABOUT THE SUN. MAKE SENSE?

NO. CAN I DRIVE ANYWAY?

NOT A CHANCE.

I WAS THINKING MORE ALONG THE LINES OF... *ZEUS'S* KID. YEAH! SHE'LL DO PERFECTLY.

OH...UH...THANKS, LORD APOLLO, BUT I'D *REALLY* RATHER NOT.

NONSENSE. ALL YOU NEED TO KNOW IS *SPEED* EQUALS *HEAT.* SO START OFF SLOW, AND MAKE SURE YOU'VE GOT GOOD ALTITUDE BEFORE YOU REALLY OPEN HER UP.

YOU DON'T UNDERSTAND. I'M--

AW, YOUR OLD MAN IS *LORD OF THE SKY.*

YOU'LL BE A NATURAL. TRUST ME.

WARNING STUDENT DRIVER

SPLOOOSH

TWO MINUTES AND FIVE HUNDRED MILES LATER.

NOTE TO SELF: DO *NOT* →*hrk*← LET THALIA DRIVE.

WHOA. IS THERE *LAVA* COMING OUT OF THAT CLIMBING WALL?

YEAH. IT PROVIDES A LITTLE EXTRA CHALLENGE.

COME ON, NICO. WE NEED TO REPORT TO CHIRON. HE'S A... WELL, YOU'LL SEE.

--THEN APOLLO BROUGHT US HERE, AND ARTEMIS LEFT FOR HER HUNT. WE'RE NOT SURE WHAT DOOMSDAY MONSTER THE MANTICORE WAS TALKING ABOUT.

OR WHAT HAPPENED TO ANNABETH...

WE SHOULD LAUNCH A SEARCH PARTY FOR ANNABETH IMMEDIATELY.

I'LL GO.

CERTAINLY NOT. THE POSSIBILITY IS VERY GREAT THAT THIS ANNIE BELL GIRL IS -≻yawn≺- ALREADY DEAD.

ANNABETH.

SHE MAY YET BE ALIVE, MR. D.

SHE'S VERY BRIGHT. IF OUR ENEMIES HAVE HER, SHE WILL TRY TO PLAY FOR TIME. SHE MAY EVEN PRETEND TO COOPERATE WITH THEM.

IF SHE IS-- AGAINST ALL ODDS-- ALIVE, THEN SHE WILL HAVE TO BE CLEVER ENOUGH TO ESCAPE ON HER OWN.

YOU'RE GLAD TO LOSE ANOTHER CAMPER! YOU'D LIKE IT IF WE ALL DISAPPEARED!

YOU KNOW, JUST BECAUSE YOU WERE SENT HERE TO BE CAMP DIRECTOR AS PUNISHMENT, THAT DOESN'T MEAN YOU HAVE TO BE A LAZY JERK!

MIND YOURSELF, BOY, OR--

NO WAY!

YOU'RE DIONYSUS, THE WINE DUDE!

I SHOWED HIM THE ORIENTATION VIDEO, SIR. HE'S SHOCKINGLY... NOT SHOCKED.

I'VE GOT YOUR HOLOFOIL CARD, TOO.

EVEN THOUGH YOU ONLY HAVE, LIKE, FIVE HUNDRED ATTACK POINTS, AND EVERYONE THINKS YOU'RE THE *LAMEST GOD EVER*, I THINK YOUR POWERS ARE TOTALLY SWEET!

AH. WELL, THAT'S GRATIFYING.

PERCY, PERHAPS YOU SHOULD MAKE YOUR EXIT. *BEFORE* MR. D REMEMBERS THAT YOU INSULTED HIM.

YOU AND THALIA GO TO YOUR CABINS AND REST. I'LL MAKE AN ANNOUNCEMENT THAT THERE WILL BE A GAME OF CAPTURE THE FLAG.

CAPTURE THE FLAG? BUT WHAT ABOUT ANNABETH?

WE NEED TO DO SOMETHING!

THE GAME IS A TRADITION. A FRIENDLY MATCH, WHENEVER THE HUNTERS COME TO VISIT.

YEAH. I BET IT'S *REAL* FRIENDLY.

THANKS FOR THE PHONE, DAD.

I COULD USE A LITTLE CHEERING UP.

SHOW ME TYSON AT THE FORGES OF THE CYCLOPES.

PLEASE HOLD.

BROTHER!

HEY, BIG GUY! HOW'S YOUR INTERNSHIP GOING?

I LOVE THE JOB! WE ARE ARMING THE MERMAIDS NOW. THEY NEED A THOUSAND MORE SWORDS BY TOMORROW.

I MADE THIS ONE ALL BY MYSELF. LOOK!

NICE ONE!

HOW'S DAD? YOU GET TO TALK TO HIM MUCH?

CLANK

CLINK

NO. DADDY IS VERY BUSY. WORRIED ABOUT THE WAR.

OLD SEA SPIRITS, AIGAIOS AND OCEANUS, ARE MAKING TROUBLE. THEY PROTECT THE BAD BOAT, TOO.

YES. THE OLD SPIRITS MAKE IT HARD TO FIND, OTHERWISE DADDY WOULD SMASH IT.

LUKE'S BOAT? THE PRINCESS ANDROMEDA?

BUT DON'T WORRY. IT'S GOING TO THE PANAMA CANAL NOW. VERY FAR AWAY FROM YOU.

PANAMA? WHAT'S IT DOING--?

GOT TO GET BACK TO WORK, BROTHER. BOSS WILL GET ANGRY.

SAY HELLO TO ANNABETH!

RIGHT.

BELIEVE ME, I WISH I COULD.

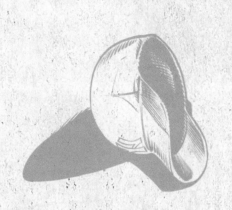

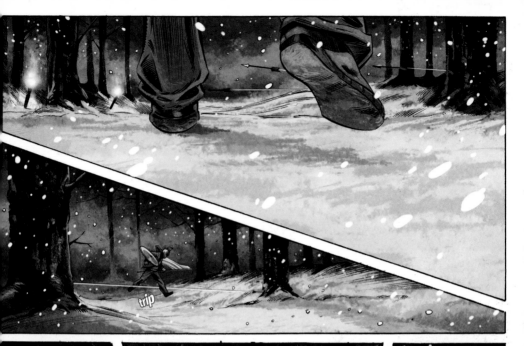

NO!

OUT OF MY WAY!

~whuff~

GO ZOË!

THE HUNTERS ARE VICTORIOUS.

FOR THE FIFTY-SIXTH TIME IN A ROW....

WHAT IN THE *NAME OF THE GODS* WERE YOU THINKING, PERCY?!

I GOT THE FLAG! I SAW A *CHANCE,* AND I TOOK IT!

YOU MEAN YOU SAW A CHANCE TO *GO SOLO!* GOOD THING THIS WAS ONLY A GAME, OR WE MIGHT'VE LOST SOMEONE.

AGAIN!

ZZAP

ARGH!

SORRY... I DIDN'T MEAN TO...

-gasp-

SPLOOSH!

YEAH. *ME NEITHER.*

I AM THE SSSPIRIT OF DELPHI, SPEAKER OF THE PROPHECIES OF PHOEBUSSS APOLLO, SLAYER OF THE MIGHTY PYTHON.

APPROACH SEEKER, AND ASSSK.

WHAT MUST I DO TO HELP MY GODDESS?

FIVE SHALL GO WESSST TO THE GODDESS IN CHAINS, ONE SHALL BE LOSSST IN THE LAND WITHOUT RAIN.

THE BANE OF OLYMPUSSS SHOWS THE TRAIL—

—CAMPERS AND HUNTERS COMBINED PREVAIL.

THE TITAN'S CURSE MUSSST ONE WITHSTAND, AND ONE SHALL PERISH BY A PARENT'S HAND.

THERE IS NO TIME FOR TALK. 'TIS AS I HAVE DREAMED--ARTEMIS IS BEING HELD HOSTAGE. WE MUST FIND HER AND FREE HER.

I WILL DEPART WITH THE HUNTERS AT ONCE.

YOU HAD A DREAM? BECAUSE I--

YOU'RE MISSING SOMETHING, *AS USUAL*, ZOË. "CAMPERS AND HUNTERS COMBINED PREVAIL." WE'RE SUPPOSED TO DO THIS *TOGETHER*.

I DON'T LIKE IT EITHER, BUT YOU KNOW PROPHECIES. YOU WANT TO FIGHT AGAINST ONE?

DOES ANYONE KNOW WHAT THE "BANE OF OLYMPUS" IS? SOUNDS KIND OF *NOT-GOOD*.

I HAVE HUNTED AT LADY ARTEMIS'S SIDE FOR MANY YEARS, YET I HAVE NO IDEA WHAT THIS BEAST MIGHT BE.

WELL, DON'T LOOK AT ME. I'M A *YOUNG* GOD, REMEMBER?

I DON'T KEEP TRACK OF ALL THOSE ANCIENT MONSTERS. IT MAKES FOR TERRIBLE PARTY CONVERSATION.

TYPHON AND KETO ARE CERTAINLY BANES OF OLYMPUS, BUT THEY ARE BOTH SEA MONSTERS THE SIZE OF SKYSCRAPERS. IF THEY WERE STIRRING, POSEIDON WOULD ALREADY HAVE SOUNDED THE ALARM.

I FEAR THE ORACLE SPOKE OF SOMETHING MORE ELUSIVE. AND *POWERFUL*.

TIME IS ALREADY SHORT. FIVE DAYS FROM NOW IS DECEMBER 21ST, THE WINTER SOLSTICE. ARTEMIS *MUST* BE PRESENT AT THE COUNCIL.

NOW, WHO WILL GO ON THIS QUEST?

THE ORACLE SAID "FIVE WILL GO WEST."

!HOW ABOUT THREE HUNTERS AND TWO FROM CAMP HALF-BLOOD? THAT SEEMS FAIR.

SHE IS THE MOST *VOCAL PROPONENT* OF ACTION AGAINST KRONOS'S ARMIES. IF SHE IS ABSENT, THE GODS WILL DECIDE NOTHING. AND WE WILL LOSE ANOTHER YEAR OF WAR PREPARATIONS.

SO BE IT. PHOEBE IS OUR BEST TRACKER. I WILL TAKE HER.

I ALSO WISH BIANCA TO GO.

SHE MAY BE OUR NEWEST, BUT THERE IS NO BETTER WAY FOR HER TO PROVE HERSELF.

AND FOR CAMPERS?

ME! YOU'LL NEED A SATYR'S SENSES, AND I'VE BEEN WORKING ON MY WOODLAND MAGIC.

AND MAYBE I CAN FIND SOME CLUES ABOUT *PAN.* THE TRAIL HAS GONE COLD SINCE LAST SUMMER...

I'LL GO.

I'VE GONE UP AGAINST MORE THAN MY SHARE OF MONSTERS. MY BATTLE EXPERIENCE WILL COME IN HANDY.

HOLD ON A SEC. ZOË ISN'T THE ONLY ONE WITH DREAMS. I HAD A REAL *DOOZY* THE OTHER NIGHT. I'M NOT SURE WHAT IT MEANT, BUT I KNOW ANNABETH NEEDS HELP.

I WANT IN ON THIS QUEST, TOO!

OH, RIGHT. I DIDN'T MEAN...

PERCY SHOULD GO IN MY PLACE. ABSOLUTELY.

ABSOLUTELY *NOT*. I FORBID IT. HE IS A BOY, AND I WILL NOT HAVE HUNTERS TRAVELING WITH A BOY.

WHAT? YOU WERE JUST ABOUT TO LET *GROVER* GO!

HE IS A SATYR. HE IS NOT TECHNICALLY A BOY.

I INSIST UPON THIS.

I WILL TAKE A SATYR IF I MUST, BUT *NOT* A MALE HALF-BLOOD.

SO BE IT. THALIA AND GROVER WILL ACCOMPANY ZOË, BIANCA, AND PHOEBE.

WHO MADE *HER* BOSS? CHIRON, TELL HER I CAN GO!

THE QUEST IS FOR ARTEMIS. THE HUNTERS SHOULD BE ALLOWED TO CHOOSE THEIR COMPANIONS.

YOU SHALL LEAVE AT FIRST LIGHT.

AND MAY THE GODS BE WITH YOU.

I'M SORRY, PERCY.

I WAS SO FOCUSED ON SEARCHING FOR PAN. I WASN'T THINKING... BUT I PROMISE, I'LL LOOK EVERYWHERE FOR ANNABETH.

IF I CAN FIND HER, I WILL.

I KNOW. THANKS.

I KNOW YOU'RE DISAPPOINTED, CHILD.

THALIA WOULD NOT HAVE BEEN MY FIRST CHOICE TO GO ON THIS QUEST. SHE ACTS WITHOUT THINKING. SHE IS TOO SURE OF HERSELF.

THEN WHY DIDN'T YOU SPEAK UP FOR ME?

YOU AND THALIA ARE MUCH ALIKE. THE DIFFERENCE IS YOU ARE LESS SURE OF YOURSELF THAN THALIA. THAT COULD BE GOOD OR BAD.

BUT ONE THING I CAN SAY WITH CERTAINTY: *BOTH* OF YOU TOGETHER WOULD BE A DANGEROUS THING.

WE COULD HANDLE IT.

THE WAY YOU HANDLED IT AT THE CREEK TONIGHT?

CALL YOUR MOTHER AND TELL HER YOU'LL BE HOME FOR THE HOLIDAYS. SHE WILL APPRECIATE THE NEWS.

THE QUEST IS IN ABLE HANDS. IF WE NEED YOU--

"--WE'LL CALL."

THUMP THUMP

YO, BOSS!

BLACKJACK? IT'S THE MIDDLE OF THE NIGHT. YOU'RE SUPPOSED TO BE IN THE STABLES.

MEH. YOU SEE CHIRON STAYING IN THE STABLES?

WELL... NO.

EXACTLY.

LISTEN, THERE'S A LITTLE SEA FRIEND THAT NEEDS YOUR HELP. I TOLD THE HIPPOCAMPI I'D COME GET YOU.

AGAIN?

SORRY, BOSS. WHO ELSE AM I GONNA TELL? YOU'RE THE ONLY ONE AROUND HERE THAT SPEAKS HORSE.

RIGHT. ONE OF THE PERKS OF MY DAD BEING THE GUY WHO CREATED HORSES OUT OF SEA FOAM.

I'LL BE SURE TO THANK HIM FOR *THAT* ONE.

AND DO ME A FAVOR, WILL YOU? STOP CALLING ME "BOSS."

I KNOW YOU THINK I GOT THE CENTAURS TO STORM LUKE'S SHIP LAST SUMMER AND HELP YOU GO FREE, BUT THAT WAS ALL CHIRON'S DOING. REALLY.

WHATEVER YOU SAY, BOSS. YOU'RE THE MAN. YOU'RE MY NUMBER ONE.

HERE YOU GO, BOSS. STRAIGHT DOWN ABOUT ONE HUNDRED FEET.

PERFECT. SHOULD BE NICE AND *WARM* DOWN THERE.

MOO!

NICE COW. YOU STAY OUT OF TROUBLE NOW, BESSIE.

Thank you, lord!

NO PROBLEM. IT'S NICE TO KNOW I CAN STILL SAVE *SOMETHING*.

BUT HOW DID IT HAPPEN?

A FOOLISH PRANK BY THOSE *CURSED* STOLL BROTHERS FROM THE HERMES CABIN. IT APPEARS THEY DO NOT ADMIRE PHOEBE'S PROWESS AT CAPTURE THE FLAG.

SHE WILL BE BEDRIDDEN WITH HIVES FOR WEEKS. THERE IS NO WAY SHE CAN TAKE PART IN THE QUEST. IT IS UP TO ME...AND THEE.

BUT THE PROPHECY... IF PHOEBE CAN'T GO, WE ONLY HAVE *FOUR*. WE'LL HAVE TO PICK SOMEONE ELSE.

THERE IS NO TIME. WE MUST LEAVE AT FIRST LIGHT. THAT IS IMMEDIATELY.

YOU SHOULD TELL THALIA THE REST OF YOUR DREAM.

IF YOUR SUSPICIONS ABOUT THE GENERAL ARE TRUE--

I HAVE *THY WORD* NOT TO TALK ABOUT THAT.

NOW COME. DAWN IS BREAKING.

SO WHAT ARE WE WAITING FOR?

NICO? WHAT ARE YOU DOING HERE?

SPYING, SAME AS YOU.

YOU HEARD BIANCA. THEY NEED OUR HELP. SO LET'S FOLLOW THEM.

I KNOW WHAT YOU'RE THINKING. IF BIANCA WAS MY SISTER, I'D BE THINKING THE SAME THING. BUT YOU CAN'T GO WITH THEM. YOU'RE TOO YOUNG.

BESIDES, IF THEY CATCH YOU-- AND THEY **WILL** CATCH YOU-- THEY'LL JUST SEND YOU BACK HERE.

MAYBE. BUT...**YOU** CAN GO!

THAT HAT. IT MAKES YOU **INVISIBLE**, RIGHT? LIKE YOUR FRIEND, ANNABETH, WHEN SHE SURPRISED THE MANTICORE.

SO YOU CAN FOLLOW THEM, ALL INVISIBLE-LIKE. I WON'T TELL ANYONE WHERE YOU WENT. I SWEAR!

YOU'RE PLANNING TO GO ANYWAY, AREN'T YOU?

YEAH...I HAVE TO HELP THEM, EVEN IF THEY DON'T WANT ME TO.

THEN GO! YOU CAN KEEP AN EYE ON MY SISTER, TOO.

AW, JEEZ. I CAN'T--

SHE'LL BE SAFE WITH YOU AROUND. I **KNOW** SHE WILL!

GOOD LUCK, PERCY! AND THANKS!

I'LL DO MY BEST.

NOW LISTEN, ABOUT CHIRON--

DON'T WORRY, I'LL MAKE UP SOMETHING. I'M GOOD AT THAT.

NOW, GO ON!

NOW WHAT?

IF I WAS GUESSING, BOSS, I'D SAY YOU NEED A GETAWAY HORSE.

YOU INTERESTED?

PERHAPS. BUT *I* HAVE BEEN DRIVING SINCE AUTOMOBILES WERE INVENTED.

I MAY NOT HAVE DONE SO HOT WITH THE SUN BUS, BUT WE'RE GOING TO GET ARRESTED WITH YOU DRIVING, ZOË.

I LOOK CLOSER TO SIXTEEN THAN YOU DO.

SORRY FOR THE LONG FLIGHT. I DIDN'T THINK THEY'D GO SO FAR WITHOUT STOPPING.

IT'S NOTHING. ⁓HUFF⁓ ⁓HUFF⁓ I CAN GO ALL DAY. ⁓HUFF⁓

NO, YOU'VE DONE ENOUGH.

GO BACK TO CAMP AND GET SOME REST. I'LL BE FINE.

REST I CAN DO. BUT BE CAREFUL, BOSS. I GOT A FEELING THEY DIDN'T COME HERE TO MEET ANYTHING FRIENDLY AND HANDSOME LIKE ME.

I'M NOT SURE *WHAT* THEY'RE DOING HERE. THE ORACLE SAID TO GO *WEST*, NOT SOUTH.

WHATEVER IT IS, I NEED TO FIND OUT.

YES. I KNOW WHERE THE ROOM IS.

NATIONAL MUSEUM OF NATURAL HISTORY.

REPORT, THORN.

THEY ARE AT THE AIR AND SPACE MUSEUM, GENERAL.

THERE ARE FOUR OF THEM: THE SATYR, ZEUS'S SPAWN, AND TWO HUNTERS. ONE OF THEM WEARS A SILVER CIRCLET.

THAT ONE I KNOW.

LET ME TAKE THEM. I'LL END THIS.

PATIENCE, LUKE. THEY'LL HAVE THEIR HANDS FULL.

I'VE SENT A LITTLE *PLAYMATE* TO KEEP THEM COMPANY.

I THOUGHT I WAS TO FINISH THEM. YOU SAID I WOULD HAVE REVENGE. A COMMAND OF MY OWN!

BAH! I AM LORD KRONOS'S SENIOR COMMANDER, AND I WILL SELECT LIEUTENANTS WHO GET RESULTS.

I SENT YOU TO CAPTURE A CHILD OF THE THREE ELDER GODS, AND YOU BROUGHT ME A *SCRAWNY CHILD OF ATHENA!*

IT IS ONLY BECAUSE OF LUKE THAT OUR PLAN WAS SALVAGED AT ALL.

NOW, LET ME SHOW YOU HOW WE WILL END THEIR FOOLISH QUEST.

DINOSAUR TEETH. HA! THOSE FOOLISH CURATORS DON'T EVEN KNOW THEY HAVE *DRAGON TEETH* IN THEIR COLLECTION.

AND NOT JUST ANY TEETH. THEY COME FROM THE ANCIENT *SYBARIS* HERSELF!

THEY WILL DO NICELY INDEED.

SOON, LUKE, WE WILL COMMAND SOLDIERS THAT WILL MAKE THAT ARMY ON YOUR LITTLE BOAT LOOK INSIGNIFICANT.

RISE! IT IS TIME TO REPORT FOR DUTY.

THE SCENT! BRING IT QUICKLY.

HERE IT ISSS, GENERAL.

EXCELLENT. ONCE MY WARRIORS CATCH THE SCENT, THEY WILL PURSUE ITS OWNER RELENTLESSLY.

NOTHING CAN STOP THEM-- NO WEAPONS KNOWN TO HALF-BLOODS OR HUNTERS.

BREATHE DEEPLY, SOLDIER.

TEAR ITS OWNER, AND ALL WHO TRAVEL WITH HER, TO SHREDS.

OH... UH...HEY.

WHAT?!

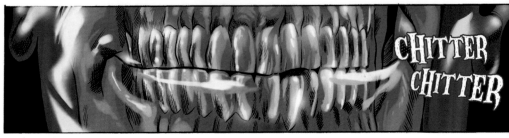

I'M PRETTY SURE THIS IS WHERE ARTEMIS'S TRAIL LEADS. THERE'S A POWERFUL MONSTER SCENT.

SHE MUST'VE STOPPED HERE LOOKING FOR THE MYSTERY DOOMSDAY MONSTER.

HEY!

PERCY! THANK GOODNESS!

YOU! HOW *DARE* YOU SHOW THY FACE HERE? YOUR PRESENCE IS FORBIDDEN!

WHAT IS IT WITH YOU, ZOË? BOYS DON'T REALLY HAVE *COOTIES*, YOU KNOW.

LISTEN. *LUKE* IS HERE. DR. THORN AND THE GENERAL, TOO.

THE GENERAL IS *HERE*? THAT IS IMPOSSIBLE.

YOU MUST HAVE SEEN AN IRIS MESSAGE, OR SOME OTHER ILLUSION.

IRIS MESSAGES DON'T GROW *SKELETON WARRIORS* FROM DRAGON TEETH.

WHAT? HOW MANY?

SIX, I THINK. AND THAT'S NOT ALL. HE SAID HE WAS SENDING A "PLAYMATE" TO DISTRACT YOU OVER HERE.

UM, GUYS...?

I THINK I KNOW WHAT HE MEANT.

ROAR

THE *NEMEAN LION!*

SEPARATE! WE MUST ATTACK IT FROM ALL SIDES.

Z-ZAT

TRY TO FLANK IT!

HI-YAH!

WHUMP

THAT WAS AN...INTERESTING STRATEGY.

HEY, IT WORKED.

TAKE THE BEAST'S PELT. IT IS RIGHTLY THINE.

NOT MY USUAL FASHION.

UH-OH.

MORE TROUBLE COMING.

DOESN'T LOOK LIKE WE CAN GET BACK TO THE VAN WITHOUT THEM SEEING. WE NEED TO FIND ANOTHER WAY WEST.

YOU GUYS GO AHEAD. IT'S ME THEY'RE HUNTING.

NO. WE GO TOGETHER. I DO NOT LIKE IT, BUT YOU ARE PART OF THIS QUEST NOW. YOU ARE THE FIFTH MEMBER--

"--AND WE ARE NOT LEAVING ANYONE BEHIND."

~snort~
~zzzzz~

YOU SHOULD BE SLEEPING LIKE THE OTHERS.

CAN'T DREAM IF YOU DON'T SLEEP.

DREAMS LIKE A PODCAST,

DOWNLOADING TRUTH TO MY EARS.

THEY TELL ME COOL STUFF.

APOLLO?

shhh. I'M INCOGNITO.

ZEUS INSISTS ON CERTAIN RULES. HANDS OFF, WHEN THERE'S A HUMAN QUEST. BUT NOBODY MESSES WITH MY BABY SIS. *NOBODY.*

SO YOU'RE GOING TO HELP US, THEN? WHERE IS ARTEMIS? AND ANNABETH?

I KNOW A LOT, AND I SEE A LOT, BUT I DON'T KNOW THAT.

THEY'RE... CLOUDED FROM ME. I DON'T LIKE IT.

WHAT ABOUT THE MONSTER? DO YOU KNOW WHAT IT IS?

NO. BUT THERE IS ONE WHO MIGHT. GO TO THE WATERFRONT IN SAN FRANCISCO AND FIND NEREUS, THE OLD MAN OF THE SEA.

HE KNOWS THINGS THAT ARE HIDDEN EVEN FROM MY ORACLE.

BUT IT'S *YOUR* ORACLE! DON'T YOU KNOW WHAT THE PROPHECY MEANS?

hmph. MIGHT AS WELL ASK AN ARTIST TO EXPLAIN HIS ART. IT DEFEATS THE PURPOSE. THE MEANING IS ONLY CLEAR THROUGH THE SEARCH.

AH, LOOK AT THE TIME. GOTTA RUN.

TAKE CARE, KID. I DOUBT I'LL BE ABLE TO RISK HELPING YOU AGAIN.

WHAT'S GOING ON?

~yawn~

WERE YOU JUST TALKING TO YOURSELF?

WAIT. ARE THOSE MOUNTAINS? AS IN THE *ROCKY MOUNTAINS*? HOW LONG WAS I ASLEEP?

JUST A COUPLE OF HOURS.

I GUESS YOU COULD SAY WE TOOK APOLLO'S HIGH-SPEED "LIGHT" RAIL.

"IT'S A GOOD THING THIS QUEST HAS US HEADING IN THE SAME DIRECTION AS THE *SUN*."

SO... HOW DO YOU LIKE BEING A HUNTER?

IT'S DEFINITELY COOL. I FEEL CALMER. EVERYTHING SEEMS TO HAVE SLOWED DOWN. I GUESS THAT'S THE IMMORTALITY.

NICO DIDN'T UNDERSTAND MY DECISION, THOUGH.

YOU KNOW, IF I HADN'T MET YOU, I NEVER WOULD HAVE FELT OKAY LEAVING HIM. I FIGURED IF THERE WERE PEOPLE LIKE YOU AT CAMP, HE'D BE FINE.

WHAT'S THE STORY WITH YOU TWO, ANYWAY? YOU NEVER LIVED WITH YOUR PARENTS? I MEAN...YOUR MORTAL PARENT?

ALL WE KNOW IS OUR PARENTS ARE DEAD. WELL, *ONE* OF THEM IS, AT LEAST. WE DON'T EVEN KNOW WHO THEY ARE.

THERE WAS A TRUST FUND FOR US. A LAWYER WOULD COME BY ONCE IN A WHILE AND CHECK ON US AT BOARDING SCHOOL. THEN, ONE DAY, HE CAME AND TOOK US AWAY.

WE TRAVELED A LONG WAY. STAYED IN A HOTEL FOR A WHILE. THEN THE LAWYER CAME AND GOT US AGAIN, DROVE US TO MAINE, AND WE STARTED GOING TO WESTOVER. THAT WAS JUST A COUPLE OF WEEKS AGO.

IT WASN'T LONG AFTER THAT, *YOU* CAME TO GET US.

AND IT'S ALWAYS BEEN JUST THE TWO OF YOU? BESIDES THE LAWYER, I MEAN.

YEAH. I LOVE NICO, BUT THAT'S WHY I WANTED TO JOIN THE HUNTERS.

I WANTED MY OWN LIFE AND FRIENDS. TO FIND OUT WHAT IT'D BE LIKE TO NOT BE A BIG SISTER *TWENTY-FOUR SEVEN*.

HAS THALIA ARRANGED OUR TRAVEL?

SHE'S NOT BACK YET.

WELL, DON'T GET YOUR HOPES UP. THE CLERK SAYS THERE'S NO WAY OUT OF THIS TOWN, UNLESS YOU HAVE A CAR.

...

THE W-W-WILD...

GROVER! TALK TO ME, PAL!

YOU'D BETTER GET HIM UP. WE'VE GOT COMPANY.

HEY! I JUST--

WHAT'S WRONG WITH GROVER?

I DON'T KNOW. HE JUST KEELED OVER.

..UUUUNNNHH...

CHITTER
CHITTER

CAT

...UHHNN...

IT'S NEAR...

THE GIFT IS NEAR...

SURROUNDED.

WE'LL HAVE TO GO AT THEM ONE-ON-ONE.

MAYBE THEY'LL IGNORE GROVER THAT WAY.

YAH!

SWISH

MY ARROWS HAVE NO EFFECT!

DOESN'T LOOK LIKE MY *SWORD* DOES EITHER....

cHITTER

CHITTER

REEEEET!!

FWUMP

-:snrrt:-

RUN!

N-NO!
I DON'T--!

JUMP!

-uff-

CRACK

REEEEET!

SOMEWHERE IN ARIZONA.

THIS IS AS FAR AS THE BOAR WILL TAKE US. WE SHOULD GET OFF WHILE IT'S DRINKING.

slurp
slurp

THANKS FOR THE LIFT, PORKY!

WHERE ARE WE?

WHEREVER WE ARE, I *HIGHLY DOUBT* WE'LL BE ABLE TO FIND A RENTAL CAR.

GUYS? WHAT ARE *THOSE*?

WE ARE ON THE EDGE OF ONE OF *HEPHAESTUS'S JUNKYARDS*. IT IS WHERE HE DISCARDS ALL HIS FAILED MACHINES AND INVENTIONS.

AND THE PATH TO ARTEMIS LEADS STRAIGHT THROUGH IT.

I DO NOT LIKE THIS. LET US REST UNTIL NIGHTFALL. WE WILL CROSS THE JUNKYARD AT NIGHT WHEN IT IS COOLER.

AND WHEN WE WILL BE LESS EASY TO DETECT.

MAYBE IT WAS *THE COFFEE*. I WAS DRINKING COFFEE, AND THEN THAT BREEZE CAME THROUGH.

MAYBE IF I DRINK MORE COFFEE...

DO YOU REALLY THINK IT WAS PAN?

I MEAN, I KNOW YOU *WANT* IT TO BE.

I DON'T KNOW HOW OR WHY, BUT HE SENT US HELP.

AFTER THIS QUEST, I'M GOING BACK TO NEW MEXICO AND DRINKING *LOTS* OF COFFEE.

IT'S THE BEST LEAD ANY SATYR HAS HAD IN TWO THOUSAND YEARS. I WAS *SO CLOSE*.

WHAT I'M WONDERING IS HOW YOU DESTROYED THAT SKELETON. THERE ARE FIVE MORE OUT THERE, AND WE NEED TO KNOW HOW TO FIGHT THEM.

I DON'T KNOW...MY KNIFE IS THE SAME AS ZOË'S. MAYBE I JUST HIT IT IN THE RIGHT SPOT?

NEVER MIND. WHAT WE SHOULD DO NOW IS PLAN OUR NEXT MOVE.

WHEN WE GET THROUGH THE JUNKYARD, WE SHOULD CONTINUE WEST TO THE NEAREST CITY. THAT WOULD BE LAS VEGAS, IF I'M NOT--

NO WAY! *NOT THERE!*

NICO AND I STAYED AT A HOTEL IN VEGAS WHEN WE WERE TRAVELING. AND THEN...I CAN'T REMEMBER...

-gulp-

BIANCA, THAT HOTEL YOU STAYED AT. WAS IT POSSIBLY CALLED--

--THE *LOTUS HOTEL AND CASINO?*

YEAH. WHY?

OH, *GREAT....*

A COUPLE OF YEARS AGO, GROVER, ANNABETH, AND I GOT TRAPPED THERE. IT'S DESIGNED SO YOU NEVER WANT TO LEAVE.

THE LOTUS MAKES TIME SPEED UP, TOO. WE THOUGHT WE WERE ONLY THERE FOR AN HOUR, BUT WHEN WE WENT OUTSIDE, *FIVE DAYS* HAD GONE BY.

BIANCA, WHO IS THE PRESIDENT OF THE UNITED STATES RIGHT NOW?

FRANKLIN ROOSEVELT. WHY...?

NO. THAT WAS OVER *SEVENTY YEARS* AGO.

DO YOU REMEMBER ANYTHING ELSE ABOUT BEFORE YOU STAYED THERE? MAYBE SOMETHING ABOUT YOUR PARENTS?

YOU GUYS ARE FREAKING ME OUT. LET'S JUST *GO.*

THERE'S THE ROAD. WE MADE IT.

WHAT'S HAPPENING?

GET CLEAR OF THE MOUNTAIN! QUICKLY!

IS IT AN AVALANCHE?

NO. THE MOUNTAIN ISN'T FALLING DOWN.

IT'S STANDING UP.

CLATTER

AAAH!

CRUNCH

HI-YA!

ZZ-ZAT

MAINTENANCE

DID YOU SEE THAT HATCH? MAYBE THERE'S A WAY TO STOP THIS THING FROM THE *INSIDE*. IF I CAN--

NO.

THIS IS ALL MY FAULT. I SHOULDN'T HAVE TAKEN THE FIGURINE.

IF ANYTHING HAPPENS TO ME, GIVE IT TO NICO. TELL HIM I'M SORRY.

BIANCA! WAIT!

HEY, RUST BRAINS! DOWN HERE!

BOOOM

NO!

RRRH

BA-BOOOM

BIANCA!

TALK ABOUT *BLOWING A FUSE.*

WHERE IS BIANCA?

IT HAPPENED JUST LIKE THE ORACLE SAID: "ONE WILL BE LOST IN THE LAND WITHOUT RAIN."

BIANCA IS GONE.

OF *ALL* THE PLACES. I CAN'T BELIEVE WE'RE HERE. ANNABETH WOULD *LOVE* THIS.

I CAN HEAR HER NOW. "SEVEN HUNDRED FEET TALL. BUILT IN THE 1930S."

"FIVE MILLION CUBIC ACRES OF WATER."

"LARGEST CONSTRUCTION PROJECT IN THE HISTORY OF THE UNITED STATES."

HOW DO YOU KNOW ABOUT THIS PLACE?

ANNABETH IS INTO ARCHITECTURE. THIS IS ONE OF HER FAVORITE STRUCTURES. SHE'S ALWAYS SPOUTING FACTS ABOUT IT.

I WISH SHE WERE HERE TO SEE IT....

WE SHOULD CHECK IT OUT. SHE'D WANT US TO.

ORDINARILY I WOULD SAY THERE IS NO TIME, BUT PERHAPS WE CAN FIND SOME FOOD INSIDE.

PERCY? YOU COMING?

YEAH... UM...YOU GO ON AHEAD. I'LL MEET YOU AT THE SNACK BAR.

YOU'RE SURE ACTING FUNNY, GIRL. WHAT'RE YOU TRYING TO TELL ME...?

OH. RIGHT.

CHITTER CHITTER CHITTER

HEY!

ENTRANCE

DOES THIS ELEVATOR GO TO THE SNACK BAR?

NO. IT GOES TO THE *TURBINE* LEVEL. THE SNACK BAR IS LOCATED ON THE FLOOR WE JUST LEFT.

WEREN'T YOU LISTENING TO MY PRESENTATION, YOUNG MAN?

OH, YEAH... THE TURBINE LEVEL... RIGHT.

IS THERE, LIKE, AN EXIT DOWN THERE?

NOT UNLESS YOU'RE MADE OF *WATER*. THE ONLY EXITS ARE THE ELEVATORS.

GREAT. ON THE BRIGHT SIDE, AT LEAST THERE AREN'T ANY *CHIHUAHUAS* ON THIS ELEVATOR.

EVERYONE, CONTINUE TO THE END OF THE HALL. ANOTHER PARK RANGER WILL BE CONDUCTING THE REMAINDER OF THE TOUR.

YOUNG MAN?

YEAH?

THERE IS *ALWAYS* A WAY OUT, FOR THOSE CLEVER ENOUGH TO FIND IT.

THIS? THIS ISN'T A SWORD. IT'S A...BALLPOINT PEN.

NO, IT'S A SWORD, *WEIRDO*. HOW DID YOU GET IT PAST SECURITY?

AND WHY ARE YOU WEARING A *LION PELT*?

YOU MEAN... THIS DOESN'T LOOK LIKE A COAT TO YOU?

UH, *NO-O*.

WHO *ARE* YOU?

RACHEL ELIZABETH DARE.

NOW, ARE *YOU* GOING TO ANSWER *MY* QUESTIONS, OR SHOULD *I* CALL SECURITY?

DON'T DO THAT! I'M KIND OF... IN TROUBLE HERE.

OKAY, HOW DO I EXPLAIN THIS...?

IN THE BATHROOM!

HUH?

IT'S ABOUT TIME! DID YOU *SEE* THAT KID? HE HAD A SWORD, FOR PETE'S SAKE. YOU SECURITY GUYS LET A *SWORD-SWINGING LUNATIC* INSIDE A NATIONAL LANDMARK?!

CHITTER CHITTER CHITTER CHITTER

HE RAN THAT WAY. YOU BETTER CATCH HIM BEFORE HE *KILLS SOMEBODY*. JEEZ!

ALL CLEAR. YOU'D BETTER HURRY. THEY'LL BE BACK BEFORE TOO LONG.

I OWE YOU ONE, RACHEL ELIZABETH DARE.

NO PROBLEM. I KIND OF HAVE A RULE: WHEN IN DOUBT, ALWAYS SIDE WITH THE PERSON THAT STILL HAS SKIN ON HIS FACE.

WHAT'S YOUR NAME, ANYWAY?

PERCY--

GOTTA GO!

WHAT KIND OF NAME IS *PERCY GOTTA-GO*?

THERE'S NO WAY OUT.

FOUR AGAINST FIVE.

AND *THEY* CANNOT DIE.

IT'S BEEN NICE ADVENTURING WITH YOU GUYS.

"THERE IS ALWAYS A WAY OUT, FOR THOSE CLEVER ENOUGH TO FIND IT."

THALIA! PRAY TO YOUR DAD. ASK HIM FOR HELP.

WHY? HE NEVER ANSWERS.

JUST *DO IT!* I THINK IT'LL BE DIFFERENT THIS TIME.

SAYS WHO?

WHAT DO YOU HAVE TO LOSE?

FATHER? WE COULD USE A LITTLE HELP HERE...IF YOU DON'T MIND.

SEE? I TOLD YOU, HE *NEVER* ANSW--

WH--?

WHOA!

MAN, IT FEELS GOOD TO STRETCH MY WINGS!

A-ARE WE VERY H-HIGH?

KIND OF. WHAT'S THE BIG DEAL?

I'M AFRAID OF HEIGHTS, OKAY? I DON'T LIKE TO FLY!

BUT YOUR DAD IS, LIKE, LORD OF THE SKY.

JUST DON'T TELL ANYONE! PLEASE?

DON'T WORRY, YOUR SECRET IS SAFE WITH ME.

SO, WHERE TO?

SAN FRANCISCO. THE WATERFRONT.

YOU HEAR THAT, CHUCK? WE'RE HEADED TO FRISCO!

OH, I AM SO THERE. PARTY!

SAN FRANCISCO.

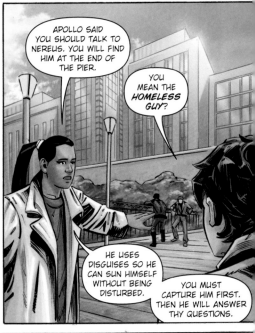

APOLLO SAID YOU SHOULD TALK TO NEREUS. YOU WILL FIND HIM AT THE END OF THE PIER.

YOU MEAN THE *HOMELESS GUY?*

HE USES DISGUISES SO HE CAN SUN HIMSELF WITHOUT BEING DISTURBED.

YOU MUST CAPTURE HIM FIRST. THEN HE WILL ANSWER THY QUESTIONS.

GOTCHA!

HELP!

I DON'T HAVE ANY MONEY, I SWEAR!

JUST *HOLD STILL,* WILL YOU? I DON'T WANT YOUR MONEY. I'M A HALF-BLOOD, AND I NEED ANSWERS!

A HERO? *BLAST!* WHY DOES YOUR SORT ALWAYS PICK ON ME?

-:groan:- VERY WELL.

DO YOU YIELD?

THE NORMAL DEAL, I SUPPOSE? YOU'LL LET ME GO IF I ANSWER YOUR QUESTION?

YOU GOT HIM!

SURE. BUT I HAVE MORE THAN ONE QUESTION.

ONLY *ONE QUESTION* PER CAPTURE. THOSE ARE THE RULES.

BUT THERE'S ANNABETH, AND ARTEMIS, AND THE MYSTERY MONSTER...

ASK ABOUT THE BEAST. LADY ARTEMIS WOULD WISH FOR US TO SAVE OLYMPUS.

YEAH, ANNABETH WOULD, TOO.

-:sigh:-

TELL ME WHERE TO FIND THIS TERRIBLE MONSTER THAT COULD BRING AN END TO THE GODS.

THAT'S TOO EASY ~scoff~. JUST LOOK **DOWN**.

POP!

BESSIE? I DON'T UNDERSTAND...

SPLSH MOO!

HE SAYS HIS NAME ISN'T BESSIE. IT'S OPHIOTAURUS.

SHE'S A **HE**? AND WHAT'S AN OPHIO-THINGIE?

IT MEANS "SERPENT-BULL."

I KNOW THIS STORY. IT'S AN OLD TALE MY FATHER TOLD ME....

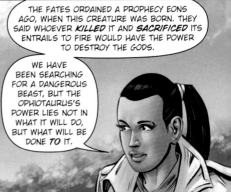

THE FATES ORDAINED A PROPHECY EONS AGO, WHEN THIS CREATURE WAS BORN. THEY SAID WHOEVER **KILLED** IT AND **SACRIFICED** ITS ENTRAILS TO FIRE WOULD HAVE THE POWER TO DESTROY THE GODS.

WE HAVE BEEN SEARCHING FOR A DANGEROUS BEAST, BUT THE OPHIOTAURUS'S POWER LIES NOT IN WHAT IT WILL DO, BUT WHAT WILL BE DONE **TO** IT.

THE POWER TO **OVERTHROW OLYMPUS**... THAT'S HUGE.

YES, IT **IS**, MY DEAR--

--AND *YOU* SHALL UNLEASH IT.

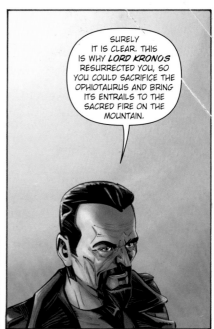

SURELY IT IS CLEAR. THIS IS WHY *LORD KRONOS* RESURRECTED YOU, SO YOU COULD SACRIFICE THE OPHIOTAURUS AND BRING ITS ENTRAILS TO THE SACRED FIRE ON THE MOUNTAIN.

THALIA, IT IS TIME YOUR FRIENDS WITNESSED YOUR *GREAT VICTORY.*

ME? WHAT ARE YOU TALKING ABOUT?

YOU KNOW IT IS THE RIGHT CHOICE. YOUR FRIEND, LUKE, RECOGNIZED IT, TOO.

YOUR FATHER ABANDONED YOU, THALIA. HE CARES NOTHING FOR YOU.

CRUSH THE OLYMPIANS UNDERFOOT AS THEY DESERVE. SLAY THE BEAST AND BECOME *MORE POWERFUL THAN THE GODS!*

I...I DON'T...

NO!

SPLOOSH!

AFTER THEM!

WE HAVE TO GET WORD TO CAMP! THEY NEED TO KNOW WHAT'S GOING ON!

GOOD IDEA.

CLINK

COLLECT CALL! CAMP HALF-BLOOD!

PLEASE HOLD.

≈ hmph ≈ AND HERE I THOUGHT I'D NEVER SEE YOU AGAIN.

WE'RE ABOUT TO DIE! WHERE'S CHIRON?

ABOUT TO DIE? HOW AMUSING. I'M AFRAID CHIRON ISN'T HERE RIGHT NOW. SHALL I TAKE A MESSAGE?

YOU HAVE TO HELP!

THE MANTICORE IS IN SAN FRANCISCO, AND SO IS THE OPHIOTAURUS! THORN IS TRYING TO GET THALIA TO SACRIFICE IT.

WELL, NOW, I HAVEN'T HEARD THE MAGIC WORD.

THE WHAT?! YOU--

HELP US, MR. D. PLEASE.

SPARE THE DAUGHTER OF ZEUS. SHE WILL JOIN US SOON ENOUGH.

KILL THE OTHERS.

FOOMP

FOOMP

NO! NOOOO!

RUSTLE

RUSTLE

FOOMP

YOU SAVED US. I CAN'T BELIEVE YOU *ACTUALLY* SAVED US.

SUCH GRATITUDE. HOW TOUCHING.

I HOPE YOU LEARNED YOUR LESSON, THERESA. POWER ISN'T EASY TO RESIST, IS IT, GIRL?

NOW RUN ALONG, ALL OF YOU. I'VE BOUGHT YOU A FEW HOURS AT MOST.

OH, I THINK THE HUNTRESS KNOWS. YOU MUST ENTER AT SUNSET, OR ALL WILL BE LOST.

BUT WHERE DO WE GO?

GOOD-BYE. I HAVE A PIZZA WAITING.

WHAT DID HE MEAN? WHERE ARE WE SUPPOSED TO GO?

THE GARDEN OF MY SISTERS.

I MUST GO HOME.

I HOPE GROVER MAKES IT BACK TO CAMP WITH THE OPHIOTAURUS. HE ISN'T EXACTLY THE BEST SWIMMER.

I PRAYED TO MY DAD FOR SAFE PASSAGE, AND EVEN OFFERED UP THE NEMEAN LION'S PELT AS TRADE.

NOT MUCH ELSE WE CAN DO....

DUSK IS AT HAND. TIME GROWS SHORT.

HELLO, SISTERS. IT HAS BEEN A VERY LONG TIME.

WE DO NOT SEE ANY SISTER. WE SEE TWO HALF-BLOODS AND A HUNTER. ALL OF WHOM SHALL SOON DIE.

GO BACK.

WE KNOW OUR FRIEND, ANNABETH, IS A PRISONER UP THERE. WE AREN'T LEAVING WITHOUT HER.

OR LADY ARTEMIS. WE MUST APPROACH THE MOUNTAIN.

THOU KNOWS HE WILL KILL THEE. THOU ARE NO MATCH FOR HIM.

LADON! WAKE!

ARE THOU MAD?

THOU NEVER HAD ANY *COURAGE* SISTER.

THAT IS THY PROBLEM.

HISS

HISS

HISS

SKIRT AROUND THE EDGES OF THE GARDEN. THE DRAGON IS TRAINED TO PROTECT THE *APPLES OF IMMORTALITY*. HE SHOULD IGNORE THEE, SO LONG AS HE THINKS I AM THE BIGGER THREAT.

IT IS I, MY LITTLE DRAGON. ZOË HAS RETURNED.

I USED TO FEED THEE BY HAND. I KNOW THOU REMEMBERS THINE OLD CARETAKER...

AAH!

HISS

ZOÈ!

NO. DO NOT CHARGE.

EVEN THE THREE OF US CANNOT DEFEAT HIM.

ARE YOU ALL RIGHT?

DID HE BITE YOU?

I AM FINE. PUSH ONWARD TO THE MOUNTAINTOP...LADON WILL NOT FOLLOW. HE WILL STAY WITH THE TREE.

THE RUINS OF **MOUNT OTHRYS**...

YES. THEY WERE NOT HERE BEFORE. THIS IS BAD.

IN THE FIRST WAR, OLYMPUS AND OTHRYS WERE THE TWO RIVAL CAPITALS OF THE WORLD.

OTHRYS WAS BLASTED TO PIECES.

IT MOVES THROUGHOUT HISTORY THE WAY OLYMPUS MOVES, BUT THE FACT THAT IT IS **HERE**, ON **THIS** MOUNTAIN, IS NOT GOOD.

THIS IS **ATLAS'S** MOUNTAIN... WHERE HE HOLDS UP THE SKY.

CORRECTION--

--WHERE I *USED* TO HOLD UP THE SKY.

HOW ARE YOU, MY LITTLE *TRAITOR*? I AM GOING TO ENJOY KILLING YOU.

YOU AREN'T GOING TO KILL ANYONE.

I WON'T LET YOU.

YOU HAVE NO RIGHT TO INTERFERE, GODLING. THIS IS A *FAMILY MATTER.* OR HAS MY DAUGHTER NOT TOLD YOU?

ZOË...?

IT'S TRUE...

...ATLAS IS MY *FATHER.*

LET ARTEMIS GO, FATHER.

PERHAPS *YOU'D* LIKE TO TAKE THE BURDEN FROM HER. BE MY GUEST.

NO, ZOË! I FORBID YOU!

I DON'T GET IT. WHY CAN'T ARTEMIS JUST LET GO?

YOU HAVE MUCH TO LEARN, GODLING. THIS IS WHERE THE SKY AND EARTH FIRST MET AND BROUGHT FORTH THEIR MIGHTY CHILDREN, *THE TITANS.*

THE SKY STILL YEARNS TO EMBRACE THE EARTH. IF SOMEONE DOESN'T HOLD IT AT BAY, IT WILL CRUSH THE MOUNTAIN AND EVERYTHING WITHIN A HUNDRED LEAGUES.

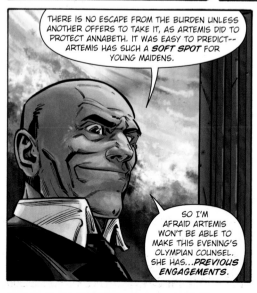

THERE IS NO ESCAPE FROM THE BURDEN UNLESS ANOTHER OFFERS TO TAKE IT, AS ARTEMIS DID TO PROTECT ANNABETH. IT WAS EASY TO PREDICT-- ARTEMIS HAS SUCH A *SOFT SPOT* FOR YOUNG MAIDENS.

SO I'M AFRAID ARTEMIS WON'T BE ABLE TO MAKE THIS EVENING'S OLYMPIAN COUNSEL. SHE HAS...*PREVIOUS ENGAGEMENTS.*

THALIA, YOU CAN STILL JOIN US. THE *OPHIOTAURUS* WILL COME TO YOU, IF YOU SUMMON IT.

DON'T YOU REMEMBER ALL OF THOSE TIMES WE TALKED? ALL THOSE TIMES WE CURSED THE GODS? IT'S TIME YOU DID MORE THAN *JUST TALK.*

MY SHIP IS DOCKED AT THE BASE OF THE MOUNTAIN. WITH YOUR HELP, KRONOS'S ARMY WILL BE READY TO STORM CAMP HALF-BLOOD.

AND AFTER THAT, *OLYMPUS* ITSELF.

DON'T, THALIA... PLEASE.

I'LL *NEVER* JOIN YOU, LUKE. I DON'T KNOW YOU ANYMORE.

THEN YOU LEAVE US NO CHOICE.

FOR ZEUS!

Z-ZZT

YAH!

YOU'LL HAVE TO DO BETTER THAN THAT!

SKRRCH

FOOLISH BOY.

ANCIENT LAWS FORBID AN IMMORTAL FROM DIRECTLY CHALLENGING A HERO.

CLACK

BUT NOW THAT YOU HAVE CHALLENGED ME--

-≥nng≤-

WHAM

--I AM FREE TO CHALLENGE IN KIND.

-≥unff≤-

RUN! A HALF-BLOOD IS NO MATCH FOR A TITAN!

NO. BUT A GOD IS.

WHISH

SMACK

SLAM

GAH!

NOW, DAUGHTER, I SHALL REPAY YOU FOR TURNING AGAINST ME.

SMACK

FINALLY. THE FIRST BLOOD OF A *NEW WAR.*

NO!

?

≈whuff≈

NO! CURSE YOU!

NO, TITAN. CURSE *YOU*. AGAIN.

EVERYONE, COME QUICK.

THE WOUND IS POISONED.

LADON BIT HER. SHE SAID IT WASN'T BAD....

PERHAPS NOT ALONE, BUT THE INJURIES SHE SUFFERED AT THE HANDS OF ATLAS ARE TOO SEVERE.

HAVE I SERVED THEE WELL, MY LADY?

INDEED. FINER THAN ANY OTHER.

REST. AT LAST.

"AND ONE SHALL PERISH BY A PARENT'S HAND." I ALMOST WISH THE ORACLE'S PROPHECY WAS MEANT FOR ME INSTEAD....

LET THE WORLD HONOR YOU, MY HUNTRESS--

--LIVE FOREVER AMONG THE STARS.

I MUST DEPART FOR OLYMPUS AT ONCE. I WILL NOT BE ABLE TO TAKE YOU, BUT HELP WILL ARRIVE SHORTLY.

YOU DID WELL, PERSEUS JACKSON. FOR A MAN.

NOW WHAT?

UH...GUYS? INCOMING.

YO, BOSS!

WE HEARD YOU GUYS NEEDED A RIDE.

THE COUNCIL HAS BEEN INFORMED OF YOUR DEEDS, HEROES. THEY KNOW THAT MOUNT OTHRYS IS RISING IN THE WEST. THEY KNOW OF ATLAS'S ATTEMPT FOR FREEDOM AND OF KRONOS'S GATHERING ARMY.

WE HAVE VOTED TO ACT.

APOLLO AND I SHALL HUNT THE MOST POWERFUL MONSTERS. ATHENA WILL CHECK ON THE OTHER TITANS TO MAKE SURE THEY REMAIN IN THEIR PRISONS. POSEIDON WILL UNLEASH HIS FULL FURY ON THE *PRINCESS ANDROMEDA*.

AS FOR YOU, YOUNG HEROES, NONE HERE WOULD DENY THAT YOU HAVE DONE OLYMPUS A GREAT SERVICE.

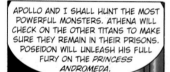

I GOTTA SAY, YOU KIDS DID OKAY. –*ahem*– HEROES WIN LAURELS––

NOW WAIT JUST A MINUTE. HAVE WE FORGOTTEN THE ORACLE'S PROPHECY?

TWO OF THESE *RUNTS* ARE DANGEROUS.

IT'D BE SAFER TO *RUN THEM THROUGH* AND BE DONE WITH IT.

THEY ARE WORTHY HEROES. WE *WILL NOT* KILL MY DAUGHTER.

NOR MY SON.

I AM PROUD OF MY DAUGHTER AS WELL, BUT ARES HAS A POINT. IT IS UNFORTUNATE THAT MY FATHER, ZEUS, AND MY UNCLE POSEIDON, CHOSE TO BREAK THEIR OATH TO NOT SIRE MORE CHILDREN.

BUT WHAT IS DONE IS DONE. THERE IS A *RISK*, HOWEVER, IN ALLOWING CHILDREN OF THE ELDER GODS TO LIVE.

MOTHER!

THALIA AND PERCY WILL NOT BE HARMED. I INSIST UPON IT.

THE *BEAST*, HOWEVER, IS ANOTHER MATTER ENTIRELY. I BELIEVE WE ARE IN AGREEMENT THAT IT MUST BE DESTROYED?

YOU WANT TO KILL BESSIE? WHAT FOR? HE'S JUST A SEA CREATURE. AND A *REALLY* NICE ONE, TOO!

YOU CAN'T!

MOO!

PERCY, THE MONSTER'S POWER IS *CONSIDERABLE*. IF THE TITANS WERE TO STEAL IT...

OR PERHAPS ONE OF *YOU* MIGHT TRY TO SACRIFICE THE BEAST'S ENTRAILS.

THE ORACLE FORETELLS THAT, ON THEIR SIXTEENTH BIRTHDAY, A HALF-BLOOD CHILD OF THE ELDER GODS WILL DECIDE THE FATE OF OLYMPUS.

FOR YOU, MY DAUGHTER, THAT DAY IS *FAST APPROACHING*.

PERHAPS NOT. MY FAITHFUL COMPANION, ZOË NIGHTSHADE, HAS PASSED INTO THE STARS. I MUST HAVE A NEW LIEUTENANT TO REPLACE HER.

THALIA, DAUGHTER OF ZEUS. WILL YOU *JOIN THE HUNT*?

DO NOT BE RASH, DAUGHTER...CONSIDER YOUR DECISION CAREFULLY.

FATHER, I WILL NOT TURN SIXTEEN TOMORROW. I WILL *NEVER* TURN SIXTEEN. I WON'T LET THIS PROPHECY BE MINE.

LADY ARTEMIS, I ACCEPT.

THE BOY IS STILL DANGEROUS. AND THE BEAST IS A TEMPTATION TO GREAT POWER.

NO. PLEASE, KEEP THE OPHIOTAURUS SAFE. I'M ONLY FOURTEEN. IF THE PROPHECY *IS* ABOUT ME, THAT'S STILL TWO YEARS FROM NOW.

TWO YEARS FOR KRONOS TO *DECEIVE* YOU.

IT IS BAD STRATEGY TO KEEP THE BEAST ALIVE. OR YOU.

I WILL BUILD AN AQUARIUM FOR THE CREATURE HERE. HEPHAESTUS WILL HELP. WE WILL PROTECT IT WITH ALL OF OUR POWERS, AND IT WILL BE SAFE.

AS FOR THE BOY... HE WILL NOT BETRAY US. I VOUCH FOR THIS *ON MY HONOR*.

ALL IN FAVOR?

WE HAVE A MAJORITY.

AND SO, SINCE WE WILL NOT BE DESTROYING ANY*ONE* OR ANY*THING*, I IMAGI WE SHOULD HONOR THE HEROE

"LET THE TRIUMPH CELEBRATION BEGIN."

YOU, UH, OKAY THERE, G-MAN?

S-SURE.

I'M JUST GOING TO KEEP D-DRINKING THESE TRIPLE ESPRESSO LATTES UNTIL I GET ANOTHER SIGN F-FROM PAN....

YOU WON'T LET ME DOWN, I HOPE.

I'LL J-JUST BE G-G-GOING.

THANKS FOR STICKING UP FOR ME, DAD. I WON'T LET YOU DOWN. I PROMISE.

LUKE ONCE PROMISED HIS FATHER THAT. HE WAS HERMES'S PRIDE AND JOY. JUST BEAR THAT IN MIND, PERCY. EVEN THE BRAVEST CAN FALL.

LUKE FELL *PRETTY HARD*, ALL RIGHT. RIGHT OFF THE TOP OF MOUNT OTHRYS. HE'S DEAD.

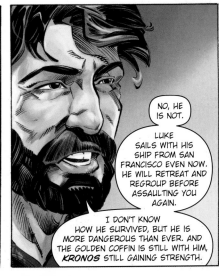

NO, HE IS NOT.

LUKE SAILS WITH HIS SHIP FROM SAN FRANCISCO EVEN NOW. HE WILL RETREAT AND REGROUP BEFORE ASSAULTING YOU AGAIN.

I DON'T KNOW HOW HE SURVIVED, BUT HE IS MORE DANGEROUS THAN EVER. AND THE GOLDEN COFFIN IS STILL WITH HIM, *KRONOS* STILL GAINING STRENGTH.

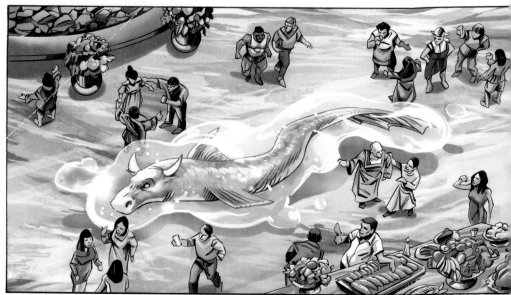

YOU DID WELL, MY SON, BUT YOUR ROLE IN THIS IS NOT YET RESOLVED. PREPARE YOURSELF. CONTINUE YOUR TRAINING, AND I KNOW YOU WILL MAKE ME PROUD.

YOUR FATHER TAKES A GREAT RISK, YOU KNOW. WISE COUNSEL IS NOT ALWAYS POPULAR, BUT I SPOKE THE TRUTH.

YOU *ARE* DANGEROUS.

FIRST, YOUR MOTHER WAS TAKEN FROM YOU. THEN, YOUR BEST FRIEND, GROVER.

NOW MY DAUGHTER. IN EACH CASE, YOUR LOVED ONES HAVE BEEN USED TO LURE YOU INTO KRONOS'S TRAPS.

THE CROOKED ONE KNOWS HOW TO STUDY HIS ENEMIES. HE KNOWS YOUR *FATAL FLAW*, EVEN IF YOU DO NOT. AND HE WILL CONTINUE TO USE IT AGAINST YOU.

YOUR FATAL FLAW IS *PERSONAL LOYALTY*.

TO SAVE A FRIEND, YOU WOULD SACRIFICE THE WORLD. IN A HERO OF THE PROPHECY, THAT IS A VERY DANGEROUS THING.

IF HELPING THE PEOPLE YOU CARE ABOUT IS A FLAW, THEN YOU'RE GUILTY OF IT, TOO.

AFTER ALL, *YOU* WERE THE PARK RANGER AT THE HOOVER DAM, RIGHT?

MARK ME, PERSEUS JACKSON. THE MOST DANGEROUS FLAWS ARE THOSE THAT ARE GOOD IN MODERATION.

EVIL IS EASY TO FIGHT. *LACK OF WISDOM...* THAT IS VERY HARD INDEED.

SHE WASN'T GIVING YOU A HARD TIME, WAS SHE?

NAH, IT'S OKAY. IF ANYBODY'S TWO CENTS ARE WORTH ANYTHING, IT'S THE GODDESS OF WISDOM'S....

COOL PARTY, HUH?

WOULD YOU...UM...LIKE TO DANCE OR SOMETHING?

WITH YOU? IN YOUR *DREAMS*, SEAWEED BRAIN.

OH, COME ON.

SALLY JACKSON. MANHATTAN'S UPPER EAST SIDE.

PLEASE HOLD.

HA-HA! SALLY, YOU'RE A RIOT! I'LL GO GET SOME MORE WINE FROM THE KITCHEN.

I'LL BE RIGHT HERE.

MOM?

PERCY?! YOU STARTLED ME. I STILL HAVEN'T GOTTEN USED TO THIS IRIS PHONE CHIRON GAVE ME.

IS EVERYTHING OKAY?

EVERYTHING IS FINE.

WHO WAS THAT...?

OH, HONEY, THAT'S JUST PAUL-- I MEAN MR. BLOFIS. HE'S IN MY WRITING SEMINAR.

WE'RE KIND OF... OH, DEAR, HOW DO I SAY THIS? WE'RE KIND OF...

MOM, ARE YOU HAPPY?

YES, PERCY, I REALLY AM. HE'S A VERY NICE MAN.

THEN DON'T WORRY ABOUT ME, MOM. I LIKE HIM BETTER THAN GABE ALREADY.

I'LL SEE YOU FOR CHRISTMAS?

ABSOLUTELY! THERE WILL BE *EXTRA CANDY* IN YOUR STOCKING THIS YEAR, TOO.

I'LL MAKE SURE OF IT.

AND PERCY? THANK YOU.

OKAY, MOM. SEE YOU SOON.

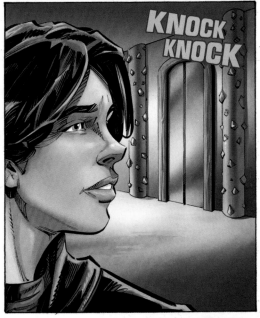

KNOCK KNOCK

HEY! ~huff huff~ I HEARD YOU WERE BACK. WHERE'S BIANCA? I WANT TO HEAR ALL ABOUT HER *ADVENTURE!*

NICO, WE NEED TO TALK....

SHE WANTED YOU TO HAVE IT. HER LAST THOUGHT WAS OF YOU.

YOU PROMISED YOU WOULD PROTECT HER.

I TRIED. SHE GAVE HERSELF UP TO SAVE THE REST OF US. WITHOUT HER, NONE OF US WOULD'VE SURVIVED THE QUEST.

YOU *PROMISED*! I NEVER SHOULD'VE TRUSTED YOU. MY NIGHTMARES WERE RIGHT!

NIGHTMARES? WHAT NIGHTMARES?

SHE'S IN THE FIELDS OF ASPHODEL, STANDING BEFORE THE JUDGES RIGHT NOW, BEING EVALUATED. I CAN FEEL IT.

YOU CAN *FEEL* IT?

OH, NO. NICO...I THINK I KNOW WHO YOUR DAD IS.

CHITTER CHITTER

NICO, GET BACK!

YOU DID IT. YOU BROUGHT THESE THINGS TO *KILL ME!*

WHAT? NO! I MEAN, YEAH, THEY FOLLOWED ME HERE, BUT *I'M* THE ONE THEY'RE AFTER.

YOU HAVE TO RUN!

NO! I DON'T TRUST YOU.

GO AWAY, MONSTERS!

RMBLLL

HOW DID YOU DO THAT...?

I WISH YOU'D FALLEN IN, TOO. *I HATE YOU!*

NICO! WAIT!

PERCY! I WAS IN MY CABIN, AND I THOUGHT I FELT AN *EARTHQUAKE.* WHAT HAPPENED?

WHY DIDN'T I SEE IT EARLIER?

SEE WHAT? WHAT ARE YOU TALKING ABOUT?

NICO. I WAS TELLING HIM BIANCA WAS GONE, AND HE SAID HE *ALREADY KNEW.* THAT HE COULD FEEL THAT SHE WAS IN THE FIELDS OF ASPHODEL.

AND THEN THE SKELETON WARRIORS WERE HERE, AND HE JUST...COMMANDED THE GROUND TO OPEN UP AND SWALLOW THEM.

ANNABETH, I THINK HIS *DAD* IS--

--HADES.

THIS IS **SERIOUS**. IT MEANS HADES BROKE THE OATH, TOO. WE HAVE TO TELL CHIRON RIGHT AWAY.

NO!

I DON'T THINK HADES BROKE THE OATH.

WHAT?

HE'S THEIR DAD, BUT BIANCA AND NICO HAVE BEEN OUT OF COMMISSION FOR A LONG TIME, SINCE EVEN BEFORE WORLD WAR II. THEY SPENT **A LOT OF TIME** IN LAS VEGAS, IF YOU KNOW WHAT I MEAN.

THE LOTUS. PERCY...THIS IS HORRIBLE. EVEN IF HADES DIDN'T BREAK THE OATH, NICO IS STILL A CHILD OF THE BIG THREE.

THAT MEANS THE PROPHECY MIGHT NOT BE ABOUT YOU. THE FUTURE OF THE GODS MIGHT LIE IN **NICO'S** HANDS.

NO. I CAN'T LET NICO BE IN ANY MORE DANGER. I OWE THAT MUCH TO BIANCA.

THE PROPHECY WILL BE ABOUT ME.

DON'T SAY THAT! YOU WANT TO BE RESPONSIBLE FOR--?

ANNABETH, I **CHOOSE** IT. I CHOOSE THE PROPHECY.

-sigh- ALL RIGHT. I HOPE YOU KNOW WHAT YOU'RE DOING, SEAWEED BRAIN.

WE HAVE TO TELL CHIRO **SOMETHING** THOUGH.

LET'S GO TELL HIM NICO GOT UPS ABOUT BIANCA AND RAN AND NOW WE CAN'T FIND

HE SPOKE! HE SPOKE!

GROVER?! *NOW* WHAT'S WRONG?

I WAS DRINKING COFFEE. LOTS OF COFFEE. AND *PAN* SPOKE IN MY MIND. THE LORD OF THE WILD HIMSELF.

HE SAID--

--"*I AWAIT YOU.*"

END OF BOOK 3.

PUFFIN BOOKS

Published by the Penguin Group: London, New York, Australia,
Canada, India, Ireland, New Zealand and South Africa
Penguin Books Ltd, Registered Offices: 80 Strand, London WC2R 0RL, England

puffinbooks.com

Adapted from the novel *Percy Jackson and the Titan's Curse*, published in Great Britain by Puffin Books
Graphic novel first published in the USA by Disney • Hyperion Books, an imprint of Disney Book Group, 2013
Published in Great Britain by Puffin Books 2014
001

Text copyright © Rick Riordan, 2013
Illustrations copyright © Disney Enterprises, Inc., 2013
Design by Jim Titus
The moral right of the author and illustrator has been asserted

Printed in Italy by Graphicom

British Library Cataloguing in Publication Data
A CIP catalogue record for this book is available from the British Library

ISBN: 978–0–141–33826–2

MIX
Paper from
responsible sources
FSC
www.fsc.org
FSC™ C018179

Penguin Books is committed to a sustainable
future for our business, our readers and our planet.
This book is made from Forest Stewardship
Council™ certified paper.